The Key to Successful Marriage

A Lifetime Commitment

With God You Can Make It!

Rev. and Mrs. Gladstone Wisdom

BK
ROYSTON
Publishing

Blessings over your life and family

Rev G Wisdom

BK Royston Publishing
P. O. Box 4321
Jeffersonville, IN 47131
502-802-5385
http://www.bkroystonpublishing.com
bkroystonpublishing@gmail.com

Cover Design: Wanda Woods

ISBN: 978-1-951941-49-9

Printed in the United States of America

Table of Contents

Acknowledgements

To our four (4) wonderful grandchildren. They are the fruit of the righteous, the second covenanted generation and the Legacy of a successful marriage. Our prayers are that they will be blessed continually and covered by the Devine protection of the Almighty God.

It is also my prayers that God will cover and bless the grandchildren of all families across the world.

Gailon & Roxanne Wisdom

Sherieka and Gariek Wisdom

ABOUT THE AUTHOR AND PREFACE

After being married to my wife, Valerie for thirty-six (36) years I have learned quite a lot about her. She is the pride and joy of my heart. Her love and commitment has brought great happiness and blessings to my personal life. Her passion for God, her dedication to the family and her love for people has impacted my life in a positive way. I am very honored to have her as my life partner. She is my best friend and confidant.

We met in 1981 at the Eastwood Park Road New Testament Church of God (Jamaica) and became acquainted with each other. We got married on February 5, 1983 and the union produced two (2) sons. We are now blessed with two (2) wonderful daughters-in-law and four (4) precious grandchildren whom we loved dearly; they are the joy of our lives.

Marriage is an institution that is ordained and covenanted by God, it should not be taken lightly or be broken. As human beings we are inherently flawed and imperfect. Valerie and I have had many challenges and many bad days, but we remain conscious of the vows we made to God, to ourselves and before the many people on our wedding day that "until death do us part." God is the God of all creation and he has made everything good, and for his glory.

God made a man and a woman to enjoy each other. According to Genesis chapter 2:18-24 God said "It is not good that the man should be alone; I will make him an help meet or a companion for him." God caused a deep sleep to fall upon Adam and he took out one of Adam's ribs and made a woman and brought her to him. Adam said "this is now bone of my bones and flesh of my flesh, she shall be called woman because she was taken out of a man." "Therefore, shall a man leave his father and mother and shall cleave unto his wife and they shall be one flesh." This explained why a man and his wife should not be ashamed when they are naked in the presence of each other, because in marriage a man and a woman symbolically are united into one.

God treats this special partnership seriously. Marriage is not just for convenience, it was not brought about by culture, it was instituted by God, and all good gifts comes from the Father above. As Christians, if we abide by the words of God, all things are possible. Solomon instructed us by his wisdom in Proverbs 3:5-6 "Trust in the Lord with all thine heart; and lean not unto thine own understanding. In all thy ways acknowledge him and he shall direct thy path."

To the many couples who have celebrated ten (10) to thirty-five (35) years of marriage and are still in love with each other; I extend heartiest congratulations. Keep the love flame burning.

I am encouraged, and I salute the many married veterans who have celebrated over thirty-six (36) years of marriage and are still saying "for better for worse, in sickness and in health, till death do us part" May God gives the grace to continue honor this sacred vow. Marriage is a commitment; marriage is true love; marriage is a God-given-gift.

Introduction

What makes a Successful marriage? Have you ever wondered why it is that some persons have a happy marriage, and some do not?

The objective of this book is to create an impact on relationships and marriages from the first stage of courtship to the commitment of marriage and thereafter. My passion is to help build strong relationships that will in turn create a more fulfilling marriage. It will provide a spiritually holistic approach to relationships; one which Jesus Christ is the center. Let us as children of God rise and take a stand against divorce and broken families. We have the will-power, the ability and the word of God to take us through, because we are more than conquerors through Christ. (Romans 8:37

It is my hope and prayers that this book will inspire you to a greater commitment and dedication to the success of your own personal life.

Gladstone Wisdom

HUSBANDS: Love your wives, even as Christ also loved the church and give himself for it.

WIVES: Submit yourselves unto your own husbands; as

unto the Lord. For the husbands is the head of the wife even as Christ is the head of the Church; and he is the Savior of the body. (Ephesians 5:22-25) Christians, this is a great mystery as Paul gives the illustrations of the oneness between Christ and the Church. He concluded in Ephesians 5:33 "Nevertheless I say, each man **must** love his wife as he loves himself, and the wife **must** respect her husband.

SINGLES: If you are planning to be married, are you willing to keep the commitment that makes the two of you one? The goal in marriage should be more than friendship, it should be oneness.   Hebrews 13:4 says "Marriage is honorable and the bed is undefiled."

Marriages have worked, Marriages can work, and Marriages still work.

There are many keys to open the door to a successful Marriage.

GOD BLESS YOU.

Rev. Gladstone J. Wisdom
Minister of the Gospel.
South Carolina.

THIRTY-SIX (36) YEARS OF MARRIAGE

We have come this far by faith leaning on the Lord.

Having been married for thirty-six (36) years I considered this a great milestone. This is not an easy Journey, but through it all we have learn to trust in God and depend upon his words. We have made a lot of mistakes; we have made many apologies to each other. We have cried and prayed together and today I can safely say God has truly brought unity in our relationship. He is the God of the Supernatural and he gives us the strength to make our marriage work.

The success of our marriage revolves around Love, Commitment, Forgiveness and Understanding. We are not perfect people, but we based our lives on Christian principles. We believe in the covenant we made with God and the pledge we made to one another in our marriage vows.

Based on the word of God in Galatians 5:23, my husband honors these words and make them an integral part of his lifestyle in our marriage. Over these years he demonstrated his love in a practical way by remembering birthdays, anniversaries and other special occasions. He often takes me out on dates and surprises me with gifts. One of his outstanding practical demonstrations is taking the responsibility of cooking the family dinner especially on Sundays when we would be getting busy to go to the house of God for worship. This practice continues even today.

I do not take this for granted, I truly appreciate his dedication to the family and I am really blessed to have such a dedicated husband. He is open-minded and has never hidden his finances from me. I can always depend on him when he gives me his words. He is very special, and I love him dearly.

We have committed to each other to live according to God's holy ordinances, to forgive one another as much as possible and to depend on God for understanding to make our relationship a success. We have built our marriage on the foundation of prayer and with Jesus Christ in the center we will be able to make our marriage much better, today, tomorrow and the years to come.

With this I can say God is in authority of our lives and his words says in Matthew 19:6 "What therefore God hath joined together. Let not man put asunder."

Valerie Wisdom

1. What is Love?

Love is the most powerful force in the world. Even the secular world realizes and acknowledges the power of Love. In many movies Love always conquerors evil. This proves just how influential Love is in all areas of Life. The Bible states in 1st Corinthians 13: "Love suffereth long and is Kind. ~Love never fails." Love is divided into several different groups. The three (3) I will focus on is Agape, Philos, and Eros. The three types should be actively demonstrated in marriages daily for proper growth and development.

(1) **Agape Love:**

This is the love of God. "unconditional Love" that is always giving and impossible to take or be a taker. It devotes total commitment to seek your highest best no matter how anyone may respond. This form of Love is totally selfless and does not change whether the Love given is returned or not. Jesus Christ demonstrates this Love for us on the cross (Romans 5:8).

(2) Philos Love:

This is brotherly Love. This type is most often shown within close relationships.

(3) **Eros Love:**

This is the feeling of arousal that's shared between people who are attracted to one another. Sexual Love is not inherently unclean or evil, rather it is the gift of God to married couples to express their Love to one another, strengthen the bond between them and ensure their survival of human race. The Bible devotes one whole book to the blessings of erotic or sexual Love (Songs of Solomon).

2. **Why Marriage**?

Marriage is a Lawful demonstration of merging both lives together with a covenant. It is a sacred vow, commitment and loyalty to each other. Based on Biblical teaching it is honorable, sacred and holy. It is the fulfillment of a lasting relationship that binds one together. There is a misconception of marriage and there are those individuals who have the opinion that to be married is to be in bondage and there are those who also share the views that all rights and freedom are taken away. This is a shortsighted view which can only lead to deception that confuses the mind of our people.

In fact, after being married for 36 years I have experienced one of the best lives that I could ever have had. This is a honorable, dignified and disciplined life that allows you to totally appreciate who you are and to the dignity of a lifetime commitment which in future create a positive impact on the quality of life and the family.

3. Communication

This is the glue that holds a relationship together. When communication between partners break down, the relationship crumbles and the marriage becomes unhealthy. Talking with your spouse clearly and frequently is the best way to keep the marriage successful. Be honest about your feelings, be kind and respectful to each other when you communicate. Part of communication is being a good listener and taking the time to understand what is it your spouse wants and need from you. Communication in marriage is like a pilot keep in touch with control of power of an aircraft. Keep your communication line clear for healthy and wholesome partnership. This is a crucial area of the marriage; lack of communication is a common cause of divorce.

4. The Effectiveness of Prayer

After living with my parents for (19) nineteen years with thirteen (13) children, I have watched them work together and take care of the family. I have never seen my father and mother quarrel. They have set a high standard on their marriage and as Christian they lived a godly life which has created a great impact on my life today.   They have lived an exemplary life together through the struggles and rigors of their relationship.

Every Sunday morning, my father, as head of the house would call the family together for prayer at 5:30 am. Every member of the family would find a place as an altar to pray, and learn to trust God individually at an early age. This was practiced regularly in the home and also at the church we worshipped. We have seen great results among the family in every area of our lives. Today the thirteen (13) children have benefitted spiritually. I am happy to say all my siblings are Christians, serving the Lord faithfully. They are married, and their children and grandchildren are beneficiary of this spiritual Legacy. My parents have made me proud. May their souls rest in peace.

Prayer is powerful, every time you pray together great things happen in your relationship. Praying together as a couple benefits your marriage in several ways. Prayer promotes unity. The day you got married you were joined together in holy matrimony (Genesis 2:24) and as one flesh. Praying together you are joined into unity with God and as a result with one another.

For a marriage to be happy and successful it has to be built on the foundation of prayer. All marriages have problems, because they are made up of two imperfect persons, but with the presence of a perfect God you will have a long and lasting result.

I know praying together works because I have seen it demonstrated in my own marriage. Over the years my wife and I have struggled with many different issues, but because of prayer we came through victoriously and are successful. Prayer changes relationships. Through the ups and downs of (36) years of marriage we have changed a lot for the better. We are not perfect, but our relationship has been good.

No matter what struggle there is in the marriage, if a couple keep praying together things will turn around for good and there will be lasting results.

5. Team Work

Working together creates a happy relationship and healthy marriage. Teamwork is a very important area in the marriage. Whether raising children, paying bills, getting groceries or house chores. This aspect in the marriage promotes bonding and trust and harmony between husband and wife and the family at large. The most successful marriages are those where a couple learn how to function as a team and lean on one another strength.

6. Complimenting Each Other

Complimenting each other is to create a deep sense of affection in appreciating the self-worth and praise of each other. Complimentary words raise the self-Consciousness and self-esteem and set the tone that each person is greatly loved and appreciated. This also raise the status of each spouse with a sense of belonging and purpose- driven lives.

Husbands and wives were divinely designed to complement each other. Wives need the respect and admiration of their husband (1st Peter 3:7) and husband needs lots of love and affection from their wives. (Titus 2:4). These should be demonstrated romantically as well - flowers, phone calls, dates, dinner time together, cards, help with chores and conversation. This will make each other happy. This will bring to each other a long and lasting marriage which is deeply satisfying.

7. Forgiveness

Forgiveness is an essential component of a successful romantic relationship. The capacity to seek and grant forgiveness is one of the most significant factors contributing to marital satisfaction and a lifetime of love.

Being able to forgive and let go of past hurt is a critical tool for a marriage relationship. This is a way to keep both parties emotionally and physically healthy. Everyone makes mistakes as both parties need to forgive and to be forgiven. No marriage relationship can be sustained Over a long period of time without forgiveness. (Ephesians 4:32) Having an unforgiven heart that is too bitter cannot love perfectly.

Couple who practice forgiveness can rid themselves of this bitterness and hurt and resolve to a happier relationship that creates a bond to a long lasting marriage.

8. Fun Time

Make fun a priority. Take time out with each other. Plan a special day and go to the beach, a day of adventure or fun evening out. Time is short, and life is busy especially with a hectic work week, accompanied with children and house chores.

Take time out and watch a football game, a cricket match or enjoy a good movie at the cinema.

Fun time with each other is rewarding. It is a good relaxer for the mind the body and the soul. This create an atmosphere for a healthy relationship and a successful marriage.

9. Preparation for Children

One must be cognizant of the fact that children are heritage of the Lord. One should be prepared with the necessary information that children are costly and they need love, affection and training for their development. One should plan adequately, prayerfully and properly for them. Be the best parent and bring them up in the administration of the Lord, this will enable them to bring added joy to the family.

Be fruitful and multiply with wisdom. Be that friend and role model for your children. Build a godly foundation for your children and they will in turn build a healthy relationship which will manifest a successful marriage.

10. Time of Worship

Make a family altar at home. Let God in your marriage. There must be an expression of true worship. This is very essential for spiritual development. In all your ways acknowledge him and he shall direct your path (Proverbs 3: 6). Your marriage was covenanted at the altar and worship sets an atmosphere for total dependency on God. Invite his presence in your home for they that put their trust in God shall never be ashamed.

Worship commands the attention of God, and with him in the family it will be a happy home.

11. Finance

This is the most critical area in the marriage. Transparency is a priority. Details and openness must be clear so that there will be no place for corruption and misappropriation of funds. There must be a clear understanding that we are one life merge together including our car, house, money or any other business one has.

Be honest to one another, be open minded, communicate with each other regularly and stay away from shady deals.

As much as possible be mindful of your family and whom you are accounted to.

12. Respecting Both Families

This is a very sensitive area of marriage. You cannot choose or refuse the family; they are the backbone of a successful marriage. There must never be at any time preferential treatment given to one side of the family, they both must be treated equally with honor and respect.

13. Sexual Relationship

Sexual relationship is very important in marriage and should not be taken for granted. I consider this moment a very important component of life. After God created man, he gave the command be fruitful and multiply and replenish the earth. Sex is similar to being hungry or thirsty and it is important that your sexual needs be satisfied. A lack of this vital ingredient will create tension, war and bitterness which leads to abuse and even death.

Sexual relationship is a holy act of God. It is divine, wholesome and pure, for both are naked and they are not ashamed (Genesis 2:25).

There are many persons today who have regrets in life. Why? Because they have committed themselves sexually outside of marriage. This is one rights that you cherish for life in marriage. May I remind you that the best thing in marriage is your sexual relationship. It is wonderful and essential for a healthy marriage. To ignore your marital duties can create problem, so keep your marriage alive.

1st Corinthians 7:3-5, reminds us of the duty of sex in marriage. God expects us to spend quality time with each other to fulfill this God given duty.

For our bodies and everything else including our sex lives must be used for the edification of both and to the glory of God.

14. Listen to Each Other's Problems

This is where the rubber meets the road. Many partners are weary and frustrated because of the insensitivity of each other. To ignore listening to each other can only create more stress and frustration.

When you listen to each other, you create a good atmosphere for reasoning and a great appetite for appreciating each other. This is a sensitive area that can help to strengthen the marriage.

You will not be able to win all conversation or solve all problems, but you must come to a conclusion and to compromise as best as you possibly can, for both must be in the best interest of the marriage.

15. Faithfulness in the Marriage

Faithfulness is part of God's character. God design and purpose for marriage is a long and lasting relationship, one of unity and togetherness.

Faithfulness does not merely mean not committing adultery, but fulfilling duties and obligations; be respectful, loving and sharing lives sacrificially with each other. Faithfulness with each other should be done whole heartedly. Being Faithful to one another, one should be truthful to his words, his promises and his vows and can be trusted always. Being faithful in the marriage; spouse should work together, work things out, forgive and overlook offenses and seek the best for the relationship.

This should be a love relationship demonstrated by God's love. A man should love his wife as Christ love his church (Ephesians 5:38).

16. The Sacredness of the Marriage Vow.

The vow is the most important law that keep the marriage together. It is a Life Covenant principle that must be observed in all circumstances. As often as possible you should renew it. Just Like an insurance policy that carries the blue print. Every statement and word play a significant role in the marriage. Seminars and workshops help to broaden your mind in a profound way. This is one of the most important area that must be kept, according to God's holy ordinance for you to experience the fullness of his blessing upon your life.

There are many challenges to face and many things can happen and also other circumstance which you have no control over, such as sickness, accident or any other disabilities, this should only serve as a positive to demonstrate your love and dedication in your marriage. When Christ is in the vessel you can smile through the storm. Face every challenge with confidence in God. He is the greatest problem solver.

17. Destruction in Marriage

Don't allow anyone to destroy your marriage. It is a known fact that there are many marriages that fall apart before the time of maturity; which is so sad. Look out for family members and friends who would like to give you advise from time to time. Make sure to analyze all information carefully. Have a mind of your own to make decisions in the best interest of your partner.

Be on your guard so that negative forces do not influence your relationship. Be open minded at all times to accept and reject. Give every support as much as possible to strengthen every fiber of your marriage. Always remember that your marriage is the first above everyone else.

Don't believe everything you hear unless it is factual and proven. Don't be quick or judgmental. Seek council whenever and wherever it is necessary.

18. For Spouse

Don't underestimate who you are. You are unique, separate and special. Elevate your self-image on a daily basis. Give yourself the best treatment. Always preferring one another in all area of your life. Your service of Love and respect is one of the most rewarding aspect of your relationship. Never take anything for granted but use every opportunity as a demonstration of your love and commitment.

Keep your marriage fresh and alive. Don't be complacent, always seek to do something outside of the ordinary. Maintain a healthy and hygienic atmosphere at all times.

Keep the bedroom clean and attractive (drapes, painting, pictures and light) this must be one of your main attraction to set the environment for a romantic display. Pay much attention to your dress code in the bedroom. You are the best advertiser of your product. There is no shame of privacy in the bedroom. You are one flesh joined together for the purpose of sexual intimacy. Keep your body fresh and clean use perfume.

19. Service of love

Don't underestimate your spouse. He or she is one of the most important persons in your life, esteem them highly. Serve each other well to the best of your ability without murmuring or complaining. Always preferring one another. Speak positive words, your self-image must be renewed on a daily basis with your mind. Always remember that negative words destroy your growth and love. Be careful how you relate to each other in public, this is a very sensitive area. Always remember that the worlds eyes are watching you. Your service of love and respect goes hand in hand. Take nothing for granted but to use every opportunity to demonstrate your sincerity of love and care. Always be cognizant of the fact that you are in a lifetime relationship that will be tested and tried. Be vigilant at all times because the adversary does not want you to succeed.

20. Distraction

Don't yield to the temptation of distraction, telephone calls and family interruption. Spend quality time together that is most comfortable to both. After a hard day's work, you need to have some time of quietness and relaxation. Share your days happening as brief as possible.

Express your happiness and delight to be back together again. Demonstrate your affection and hospitality with a refreshing drink or a hot meal then ending with a hug and kisses.

21. MARRIAGES SCRIPTURES

1) Genesis 21:21-24

And the Lord God caused a deep sleep to fall upon Adam and he slept: and he took one of his ribs and closed up the flesh instead thereof.

And the rib which the Lord God had taken from manmade he a woman and brought her unto the man.

And Adam said, this is now bone of my bones, flesh of my flesh: She shall be called woman, because she was taken out of man.

Therefore, shall a man leave his father and his mother, and shall cleave unto his wife: and they shall be one flesh.

2) St Mark 10:6-9

But from the beginning of the creation God made them male and female.

For this cause shall a man leave his father and mother and cleave to his wife.

And they twain shall be one flesh: so, then they are no more twain but one flesh.

What therefore God hath joined together, let not man put asunder.

3). Hebrews 13:4

Marriage is honorable in all, and the bed undefiled. But whoremongers and adulterers God Will Judge.

4) Proverbs 18:22

Whoso findeth a wife findeth a good thing and obtain the favor of the Lord.

5) Proverbs 19:14

House and riches are the inheritance of fathers and a prudent wife is from the Lord.

6) **Proverbs 31:10**

Who can find a virtuous woman for her price is far above rubies.

7) **Proverbs 12:4**

A virtuous woman is a crown to her husband but she that maketh ashamed is a rottenness in his bones.

8) **1st Peter 3:1 & 7**

Likewise, ye wives be in subjection to your own husbands that if any obey not the word, they also may without the word be won by conversation of the wives.

Likewise, ye husbands dwell with them according to the knowledge, giving honor to the wives as unto the weaker vessel and as being heirs together of the grace of life, that your prayers be not hindered.

9) **Colossians 3: 18-19**

Wives submit yourselves unto your own husbands as it is fit in the Lord.

Husbands love your wives and be not bitter against them.

10) **Ephesians 5:22-25, 28-29**

Wives submit yourselves unto your own husbands as unto the Lord.

For the husband is the head of the wife, even as Christ is the head of the church and he is the Savior of the body.

Therefore, as the church is subject unto Christ so let the wives be to their own husbands in everything.

Husbands love your wives even as Christ also loved the church and gave himself for it.

So, ought men to love their wives as their own bodies. He that loveth his wife loveth himself. For no man ever yet hateth his own flesh, but nourisheth and cherisheth it.

22. Here I recommend 20 simple keys that are very important to the development of marriage.

Twenty (20) Simple Keys

- Love
- Joy
- Peace
- Patience
- Gentleness
- Kindness
- Forgiveness
- Goodness
- Happiness
- Affectionate
- Long suffering
- Self-control
- Hospitality
- Respect
- Have an open mind
- Have a positive mind
- Be transparent

- Be a good host
- Preferring one another
- Keep your heart pure (Galatians 5:22-23)

23. **My Passion**

This is my passion and conviction. I am sending a message to the present and future generation, that marriage is till God's order for all generation.

There is a moral, ethical and spiritual decline in our society and the world. I am concerned as a Minister of the gospel, who have been saved at the age of 12 years old. After serving the church in most of the critical and important areas of the ministry, and have council with a lot of persons at different level; I have seen the abuse, disrespect and divorce and even death in many cases. I am fully convinced that there is a better way forward for our future generations. We must be able to distinguish right from wrong. Let us return unto God for he will abundantly pardon. Let us turn a new page and begin a new chapter of love and turn back the evil of deception that plague us for so long. Rise up and take a stand toward building successful marriages. Let me say to you it does not matter what you are going through, there are millions who have been tested and tried, but today they are still together. Your best days are ahead, you can make it under God. Be determined, be resolute, be courageous, be strong, be committed, be prayerful, be sincere, be confident and be steadfast.

In this book, I share with you some of the most important and fundamental areas that is vital for your own natural and spiritual life.

Let God bless you as you read. Be prayerful and open minded.

24. Impacting The Life of a Generation

Don't forget that your life and marriage is like a mirror that everyone can see through. Even though you are a unit you must be ready and willing to share your life's experience with others. After all is said and done you are an Ambassador for Christ. Your aim and goal is to impact others to face a challenging future. There is no success without people. Let your marriage serve as a catalyst of change for a better and caring world.

Be conscious at all times of your responsibility, your environment and your culture. You are living for one of the most important reasons and that is to serve others as an instrument to God's glory.

Our Nation and people are in high demand for quality leadership; in the home, to mentor and be role models. Use your marriage life in the best way you can to make a difference; to spread love, give hope, give counsel and advice. Be prayerful as you share with each person.

Let God be glorified in every aspect of your marriage life. If you are not yet saved and having a born-again experience, let this day be the beginning of a new life of spiritual renewal and commitment to each other.

Rev. Gladstone Wisdom   -

Wisdom keys from Married Couples

THREE (3) PRINCIPLE OF MARRIAGE

<u>Marriage at its best</u>

1. **Commitment**:

Our commitment is the glue that holds us together. Without true commitment to each other it will be hard to last.

2. **Forgiveness**:

Forgiveness is also key to a lasting marriage. No one is perfect, little things matters. We must be quick to forgive and continue to move forward.

3. **Trust**:

Trust is essential to a lasting marriage. Jealousy and suspicion have no place in a marriage. We must remember our vows before God and each other.

Lady Donna Chavis

Rev. and Mrs. Peter Garth

REASONS FOR OUR SUCCESSFUL MARRIAGE

I have been married to my wife, Flora for the past thirty-six (36) years. We got married on the 20th February, 1982. There are many things that contribute to a happy marriage, but one of the many things is to acknowledge that a successful marriage is when each person in the marriage lives more for the other person, than for himself or herself. There are some key principles and concepts that have made our marriage a success over these thirty-six (36) years. First, we accepted the **Biblical Foundation** which sees marriage as a union. We embraced the common ownership ("one flesh") principle of leaving and cleaving. A big part of the foundation is to have a proper understanding of love and submission, which came easy as a result of Christ being in control of our lives. We also recognized that marriage is a lifelong covenant and that we are required by God to keep our marriage for Him. Second, we also accepted the **Spiritual Foundation** and this involves our personal commitment to Christ, personal devotional life and growth, our ministry goals and developing biblical convictions.

The three (3) major areas which cover a successful marriage are:

1. Communication
2. Finance
3. Sex

Communication

If any marriage is going to be successful the individuals must know how to deal with negative and positive attitudes as new ones will surface. From the outset we looked at our expected roles and responsibilities which augur well planning. We had to learn how to deal with handling conflicts and differences as well as criticisms, hurts and inner healing. One of the things that I am sure made our marriage work is our acceptance of the reality that complements open the door for criticisms. In other words, it is always best to complement more than criticize. We are able to communicate well because of our understanding of peculiarities, habits and moodiness. Essentially we followed what I called the ten (10) **Commandments of Communication:**

1. Be a ready listener
2. Be slow to speak. Think first
3. Speak the truth always, but do it in love
4. Do not use silence to frustrate the other person
5. Do not become involved in quarrels
6. Do not respond in anger
7. When you are in the wrong, admit it and ask for forgiveness
8. Avoid nagging
9. Do not blame or criticize the other but restore, encourage and edify

10. Try to understand the other person's opinion

Finance

Before we got married we had a clear understanding as to how we would deal with our financial matters. For the past thirty-six (36) years has been built on trust and is has worked very well for us. We have been able to budget, manage our funds and operate on the principle that major financial decisions must be made together. If this is not done there would have been constant pressure in our marriage.

Sex

This area of marriage is very critical and in many marriages it is not talked about. Sex must never become a bargaining right in marriage. The bible teaches that in marriage the couple must understand that sex was intended by God for pleasure and not only procreation. In our marriage there was always personal convictions about sex, morality and self-control. We worked at how to keep the romance in marriage and we set aside time for vacation and just 'alone time' with each other.

Rev. Peter Garth
Pastor, Hope Gospel Assembly

"What Kept Our Marriage for 43 Years"

He whom God has joined together, let no man put asunder {Mathew 19:6} With this command I say, "Hither to hath the Lord helped us." God has placed marriage as a priority in the Bible because it is the institution where relationship and family life begins. It is the greatest of God's creation. After Adam and Eve sinned God gave some new instructions and guidelines to ensure its safety and security. One such guideline is staying together and avoiding parental or other interferences. Matthew 19:5 advises a man to leave mother and father and cleave to his wife.

Now a widow, I reflect with sincerity and deep appreciation for God's divine favor, mercy, grace, love and tremendous blessings that kept our union together. Truly the Lord's mercies and compassion did not fail and these are factors which contributed to the success of our marriage. The keys to stick-to-itiveness in our marriage was showing acts of kindness, love, and forgiveness, towards each other. These, mixed with grace, were necessary to cross over the rough patches while exercising patience and understanding. The communication key- ring kept all the keys together and actively opened and closed doors for good relationship. Our humility to acknowledge each other's strengths and weaknesses were building blocks which deepened our marriage commitment. I spent much time praying for my spouse, four children and extended families, while giving moral and spiritual support with encouragement. This was priority.

"No man is an island; no man stands alone...." We need one another and even the weakest link in a chain is important. Jesus cared about the one sheep that was missing from the hundred fold.

Fun Times: Our marriage was also bonded together by fun activities we enjoyed. My husband and I loved cricket and were both passionate about the game. Much laughter at the boundaries and victory shouts at the "outs" and "not outs." We often went to the beach with the entire family. Visits to family members who lived miles away was a pleasure and our children also looked forward to this. Honesty in confronting issues had its place and foundation in the Word of God. It was not taken lightly. The attitude of openness and integrity was instilled in the upbringing of our children. As ministers of the Gospel of Jesus Christ, we had our fair share of trials and tests but our children continue to serve in various capacities in the church and blooming where they are planted.

"Duty is ours, events are Gods" was a motto used by us in our marriage. We were committed to training our children guided by the principles of God's Words. Family worship was the gate way to discussions, concerns and finding solutions to problems, while appreciating the goodness, greatness, kindness love and mercies of God. We made it to 43 years by faith, leaning on the Lord and I am grateful. The joy of the Lord is still my strength. I continue to pray for my biological family, my grand-children, in-law's and church family. The family that pray together, stays together. He that dwelleth in the secret place of the Most High shall abide under the shadow of the Almighty {Psalm 91:1}.

Marriage is still God's holy estate and will work when guided by the Holy Scriptures, Jesus as Redeemer and the Holy Spirit as Comforter.

Rev. Veronica Ewan
Kingston, Jamaica.

Bishop Ronald Blair and Rev. Evon Blair

MARRIAGE STILL WORKS

We have been married for fifty-three (53) years. Many may wonder how so long? What's the trick? How is it that you remain so happy and together after over half a century?

The truth is, we understood that marriage was and still is a covenant. As a covenant, it should be held with high regard and should not be broken. Therefore, in spite of the hard knocks – the imperfections, the misunderstandings, the failures in our high expectations of each other, we stuck to the pledge we made, remembering that whatever negative response we made would impact the lives of the people around us.

Personally, I have always shown the deepest respect and appreciation for my husband. I have learnt the art of keeping silent. This is good medicine. My husband and I pray, read and study the Word of God and worship together. These are good 'solidifiers' for a good relationship. The other good ingredient which has kept us going for these many years is the love we have for each other. God has placed us together, and we plan to keep our relationship in good stead until Jesus comes or call us home.

Marriages can work, give one hundred percent (100%) of yourself to each other and you will be surprised how fruitful your marriage can be.

Rev. Evon Blair

LEAVE AND CLEAVE

Gen. 2
24 Therefore shall a man leave his father and his mother, and shall cleave unto his wife: and they shall be one flesh.

Herein lies the root of marriage. A man and a woman, the man subordinates his family for his wife and the process of cleaving now begins. But what is cleaving? Cleaving is; to stick with and close to, to stay with until death separates.

For any man to stick with and close by any woman, it must begin with one word, and that word is commitment.

Forty-five years ago, I made a commitment to my wife, after hearing a voice deep within me saying, "You have a good woman here, why don't you marry her and settle down?" I heard that voice more than once.

Understand carefully that I had just graduated from university with a degree and was a self-described atheist. That voice I came to realize many years later was the voice of the Holy Spirit speaking deep within me, yes God speaks to atheists as well as wicked biblical rulers. A few months later I answered the voice and did not ask my girlfriend to marry me, but told her that we are going to get married. We got married on July 15, 1973. God's grace has kept us through many storms and trials, but because of my commitment and hers, we worked on the many tribulations we encountered in marriage and overcame them. Know this for sure that every marriage must begin with commitment to each other and to the union of the marriage. We were not committed to God at that time as we were not saved, but God's mighty hand was upon our lives. God knew that over a period of time we would finally surrender our lives to Him, so His plan and purpose for our lives would be fulfilled in and through us.

Today after forty-five years of marriage, we are walking in our God mandated destiny, Pastoring, preaching, teaching and writing books about the living Word of God.
We thank God for His preservation and mercy as we are still committed to Him, our marriage and each other after forty-five years.

Hard work trumps talent when talent does not work hard!

Bishop Norman & Lady DaCosta
Miami. Florida

Marlon & Carmelita Benderson

A MATCH MADE IN HEAVEN

Carmelita and I have been happily married for over eleven (11) years.

How we met

We met at church at a Youth Ministry meeting back in March of 2000. Our relationship started out of a pure concern for her spiritual growth and development which arose when I observed her inconsistency in attendance to Sunday School. At the time we were both in our teens and were both in the same Sunday School class. I developed a concern when I saw that her attendance to Sunday School was in consistent and decided to engage her to find out what was the issues she was having. So, I engaged her one Friday evening after Youth Ministry meeting and asked her for her phone number. We subsequently had several conversations on the phone including devotional exercises and our friendship grew and blossomed.

A friendship was born

The more we communicated on the phone the more we discovered a true friend in each other. Carmelita prayed to God for a sincere friend before meeting me and I prayed to God requesting that the person he would ordain for me would become my best friend. "Friendship is a way of acting and being with someone that makes them feel valued, cared for, and respected. It's letting them know you appreciate them and care about their feelings. Being a friend means treating another with special care and kindness because they mean so much to you." Our friendship grew from strength to strength because we valued each other, we shared common interests and goals and most importantly we genuinely wanted the best for each other. Seven years after sharing in a pure friendship we got married on July 28, 2007. It was a match made in heaven.

The Secret to the longevity of our Marriage

When we look back over eleven (11) years of togetherness we see the basic ingredients that brought us together being practiced every day. Just has we started; we pray together, we plan together, we play together. This 3 p's are what has caused our marriage to remain strong and healthy. We see God has the central link that bind us together as husband and wife. Our common denominator being our friendship and with God in our vessel we have smiled and continue to smile at the storms.

Marlon and Carmelita Benderson

Milton and Altheia Wisdom

FOR BETTER FOR WORSE

We have been married for thirty (30) years and we have a beautiful daughter, Elizabeth.

Throughout our journey together, we learn about each other and about ourselves. Here are a few things we learnt:

1. It is important to apply God's word daily when you are challenge as a couple. "In all your ways acknowledge him and he shall direct your path". ***Proverbs* 4:6**
2. Talk to each other
3. Forgive quickly
4. Have a good sense of humor
5. Say I love you
6. Show Love and concern to each other-in-laws
7. Marriage is practical. Partners should help each other in their own way. For example, if taking out the garbage is your way of helping, then do that. It is the small unspoken gesture that mean the most.
8. As much as possible try not to embarrass your spouse in public
9. No matter what, never let anyone come between you and your spouse.
   1) We use three (3) P's in our marriage.
   1) Pray together
   2) Plan together
   3) Play together

We pray that you will be blessed and encouraged

Milton and Altheia Wisdom

A SUCCESSFUL MARRAIGE

We have been married for thirty-five (35) years. Having attained this success, we have built our lives on the Lord Jesus Christ. We have asked him to be the glue in our marriage, because without him we could not have been together this long.

First, we have got love and affection for each other. Second, we cultivate a mutual respect for one another and among all we trusted each other.

Communication is vital for any successful marriage and this we do each day on any given subject. We are very open, which means we keep no secrets from each other. Then comes caring and sharing which we maintain as an integral part of our marriage vow.

With these ingredients we mixed together, thus help us to maintain a successful marriage.

Morris & Rosemarie McIntyre

Kingston, Jamaica

Granville and Desserene Benjamin

A MARRIAGE MADE IN HEAVEN

We are educators in Jamaica for the past thirty-three (33) and forty (40) years respectfully. We are pleased to be given the opportunity to express ourselves through this medium.

It gives me inestimable joy to speak about our marriage. We are now celebrating sixteen (16) wonderful years. This marriage was made in heaven. God has been at the center of this marriage. Our union has produced one son. We cannot exhaust the forgiveness we have exhibited to each other. We serve each other with fervor and fortitude. We enjoy each other's company. We are extremely pleased with God with the choice he has made for us. To have it better it would have to be with our maker. Blessings.

Granville and Desserene Benjamin (Educator)

Rev. Ishmael & Charis St. Louis

THE SECRET TO A SUCCESSFUL MARRIAGE

Marriage is a covenant relationship between a man and a woman This relationship is very different from any other relationships because it was designed by God to depict his relationship with the church (body of believers in Jesus Christ).

In its design, God wanted to show the mystery of how two (2) individuals from different background can come together and be united as one flesh. Such a unique relationship is best achieved when God is placed at the center of your marriage.

This has been my experience. I have placed God at the center of my marriage and He has been helping me and my husband to resolve conflicts, and to love and care for each other.

Conflicts in a marriage are inevitable, and so a successful marriage depends to a large extent on how these conflicts are dealt with.

Charis Wisdom- St Louis

Canada

OUR MARRIAGE

We have been married for twenty-eight (28) years. The journey that we have walked on has taught us many things about ourselves and one another.

After praying about this statement, I feel there are five (5) things that will keep a marriage together:

1. **Jesus -** Because with Him direction is given. He created the unity between Husbands and wife (male & female)

2. **Love -** What is it; no matters who each facing – the hunger to hold, touch, and be together. Burn in you, Remember the date, days and first year.

3. **Finance -** Money, the abundance will make you feel like I don't need anyone. The lack of will cause one to look at others, instead of the blessings you have. Paul said in Philippians 4:11 "I have learned to be content in all things".

4. **The Holy Spirit -** Jesus said in John 14:26, The Spirit will teach and bring all things to your remembrance. Things you have seen that work and things that have torn marriage apart.

5. **Commitment -** As we have said in our vows, "till death do us part". Commitment - to do all the above as it has been said, Love will keep us together, but it also takes actions.

Pastor James & Joan Freeman

Rev. Mark & Mrs. Loraine Hardy

HARDCORE TRUTH ABOUT MARRIAGE!

1. There is nothing that threatens the security **of a wife than the thought** of **another woman competing for the attention and affection of her husband**.

Nothing is more painful. Nothing is more insulting. Noting is more belittling and degrading.

2. Marriage flourishes when the couple works together as a team, when both husband and wife

decide that winning together is more important than keeping score. Good marriages don't just happen. They are a product of hard work.

3. Your children are watching you and forming lasting opinions on Love, commitment and marriage. Based on what they see in you. Give them hope. Make them look forward to marriage.

4. Husbands: The reason why women look attractive is because someone is taking good care of them.

Grass is always green where it is watered. Instead of drooling over the green grass on the other side of the fence, work on yours and water it regular. Any man can admire a beautiful woman, but it takes a true gentleman to make a woman admirable and beautiful.

5. When a husband puts his wife first above everyone and everything except God, it gives his wife the sense of security and honor that every wife hunger for.

6. A successful marriage doesn't require a big house, a perfect spouse, a million dollars or an expensive car.

You can have all the above and still have a miserable marriage. A successful marriage requires honesty, undying commitment and selfless love and God at the center of it all.

7. Pray for your spouse every day; in the morning, in the afternoon and at evening. Don't wait until there is an affair. Don't wait until there is an affair. Don't wait until something bad happens. Don't wait until your

spouse is tempted. Shield your spouse with prayer and cover your marriage with the fence of trust.

8. The people you surround yourself with have a lot of influence on your marriage.

Friends can build or break your marriage; choose them wisely.

9. One spouse cannot build a marriage alone when the other spouse is committed to destroying it.

Marriage works when both husband and wife work together as a team to build their marriage.

10. Don't take your spouse for granted. Don't take advantage of your spouse's meekness and goodness. Don't mistake your spouse's loyalty for desperation. Don't misuse or abuse your spouse's trust. You may end up regretting after losing someone that meant so much to you.

11. Beware of marital advice from single people.

Regardless of how sincere their advice may be, most of it theoretical and not derived from real life experience. If you really need Godly advice, seek it from God -fearing, impartial and prayerful mature couples whose resolve has been tested by time and shaped by trials.

12. Dear wife, don't underestimate the power of the tongue on your marriage. The tongue has the power to crush your marriage or build it up. Don't let the devil use your tongue to kill your spouse's image, self – confidence and aspirations. Let God use your tongue

to build up your marriage and bless and praise your spouse.

Marriage is team work which works best without third party influence. Don't let others predict the fate of your marriage. Create a relationship that is unaffected by false presumptions of others.

Wishing you all a happy marriage and for those single I wish a happy relationship.

Rev. Mark & Mrs. Loraine Hardy

Rev. Errol & Heather Rattray

STATEMENT ON OUR MARRIAGE

We thank God for bringing us together to share our lives. We have been blessed with forty-two (42) happy years of marriage and continue to enjoy a very special bond. As a couple we have operated under the umbrella that God must be at the center of our relationship and this has proven to be the stabilizing factor in the relationship. Additionally, we have built our lives around some other important principles such as honesty, respect, forgiveness, trust and most of all being good friends. We have also allowed each other the flexibility to pursue and achieve their own goals and in turn offers the personal satisfaction and fulfilment which cultivate happiness. Recreation is also fundamental to a happy and successful union and we have tried to incorporate this important ingredient in our relationship. We strongly recommend these principles to young couples and persons who are experiencing challenges in their marriage.

We thank God for giving the vision to Evangelist Gladstone Wisdom to write this particular book which we believe will impact thousands across the world. Congratulations and best wishes.

Rev. Errol & Heather Rattray
Evangelistic Association
Kingston, Jamaica.

STATEMENT ON OUR MARRIAGE

Larry and I were married on November 3, 1972. After forty-two (42) years I look back and see that we were just children entering into an adult world. We struggled really bad for the first six (6) months of our marriage.

In May of 1973 our whole world changed, we accepted the Lord as our Saviour. I can't say it was an instant change in our marriage, but we started seeing things in the way we were living and we started working together to save our marriage as a Christian Couple.

Marriage is a relationship you work on every day. You commit to the Lord and each other to make your marriage work. You respect and work things out every day. Don't go to bed mad at each other. Sometimes you may have to put 50% and sometimes you might have to put 100% into your marriage, but you work together as a couple, the way God intended it to be.

Pastor Larry & Libbie Baldwin

PUT GOD FIRST

Rosella and I have been married for thirty-two (32) wonderful years. Have it all been rosy, of course not, but by far the good years outweigh the few shaky months.

What makes a marriage successful has been debated for years, but the answer lies in how individuals take seriously the sanity of their marriage vows. Rosella and I take very, very serious the part of the vow that says 'for better or worse'. Believe me in thirty-two (32) years we have had to deal with some worse, but because we always put God first, we never ever leave him out of anything we go through whether better or worse. This is why our marriage has been successful.

Pastor Joseph & Rosella James

When I thought about the title of this book, the first thing that comes to mind is my own marriage of twenty-one (21) years, did not survive the storms in the first ten (10) years. Being a child of God (Christian), I read books that would enhanced our marriage and one such book was "I Love You" by Gordon O. Martinborough. But as Amos 3:3 asked the question, **'Can two walk together except they agreed?"** and 2ⁿᵈ Corinthians 6:14, **"don't be unequally yoked."** This is to say, we must be in accordance with Jehovah wanting the same thing and doing his will together and not performing the task separate that put before us.

As I reflected on the past, I realized that this was very real and our pre-martial counselling session wasn't a rigorously one. If it was, I would not have married my boyfriend who had no interest of accepting Jesus Christ as his personal Saviour. He believed that attending church was okay for him. I fought with God in fasting and prayer and thought that me being saved, he would come after, which was not so. The final straw we separated, then divorced in the eighteen year, when it was my 50ᵗʰ birthday and that same year our daughter would become eighteen (18) years old. This has been the most grilling situation; I would not want anyone to experience. So, if I was to enter another relationship which will lead to marriage, this would be 'The Key to Successful Marriage':

- Communication on the same level
- Appreciation of each other success and not competitive to see who can achieve the most.
- United in fasting and prayer

- Plenty love
- Willing to say you are sorry and not hold a grudge
- Respectful to each other
- Supporting to each other
- Patience/Forgiveness
- Time for each other
- Trust

Rev. Wisdom, may our heavenly Father continues to inspire you to write more books.

Paula McCreath- Wright

Pastor Raphel & Shellyann Wisdom

I am honored to be allowed this space to be able to send words of congratulations to one of the world's best couple. I've been blessed with the opportunity of getting to know you both for over six (6) years and the love, affection, strength, courage, trust and respect that you both have displayed to this union. It leads a lasting impact to my life; the encouragement that marriages still last, that person of different character can come together and through love put aside selfishness and still be subjected to one partner. Your union has still offer hope to many other unions, the hope that this thing can work.

Today so many marriages have died, and this dead rate continues to rise, but like a light on dark night so is the life of your union. It continues to shine it light of hope.

Lady Shellyann Wisdom

THE KEY TO A SUCCESSFUL MARRIAGE

If Marriage is still defined as the "formal union of a man and a woman" (Oxford,2018) and referred to as husband and wife. Successful is to be defined as ..." having accomplished or achieved a desired aim, result or successful outcome" (Oxford, 2018).

So, there are three (3) fundamental questions to anyone who claims to have had a successful marriage:

1. What was the desired aim of your marriage?
2. What has been the result of that desired marital aim?
3. What are the specific keys to open the door to a successful marriage?

From a scriptural / biblical perspective, the desired aim of marriage is to ".... Leave.... Cleave... Be one flesh."

(Genesis 2: 24)

The 'Original' marital covenant or vow; exchanged at wedding ceremony, must be witnessed by a company of at least two (2) adults, states that.... To love, cherish, honor, respect.... Until death do us part...

So! One could agree that the ultimate goal of marriage is until one spouse dies!

According to Genesis 1: 27- 28, marriage was designed for his family (human-being) male and female. The same pattern for every creature; Land, water and air even to the times rain upon the earth. (Genesis 6: 19; 7 :2-4).

Hence the first key to the "Bank or Love" call marriage would be to honor God as priority. By natural occurrence the second key to a successful marriage would be the emphasis on your spouse! besides God, your spouse must feel important, knowing they are loved; (Ephesians 5:21-25, 28-30) appreciated, respected, trusted and nourished (1st Corinthians 7: 3-4; Ephesians 5: 21-25,28-30) Prayer and fasting are the third set of keys to a successful marriage. (1st Corinthians 7:5; Colossians 3: 18-19). Remember there should be no celibacy in marriage: physical intimacy is essential to marital success.

Herman's, (2011) suggests that a commitment to communication is basic to a successful marriage; both spouse listening and understanding what the other is expressing, opening up and sharing your thoughts and feelings might leave vulnerable but it's the basis for a successful marriage.

Most writings on marriage (to include the holy scripture) implies some attitudinal words, beginning with the letter 'Cc" to enhance (lubricate) the keys to a successful marriage: Compatibility consultation. (Amos 3:3) Combine, cherish, coverage, comfort, cuddle (1 Peter 4:8) Compromise and Confession.

Contributed by: Mary Ann Nicholas (Man) JP; Revd.; Dr. Resident Pastor, Master Guidance

counselor, retired education officer and college president, current school board principal/ administrator _ Wife, Now a widow- in deed, parent, grand & great grandparent ...)

LOVE AND SUBMISSION

"Husbands, love your wives, even as Christ also loved the Church, and gave himself for it." Ephesians 5:25.

Husbands have been given greater responsibility to love their wives. The standard is to love them even as Christ loved the Church and gave himself for it. Any husband who does not love his wife to the point of death has not fulfilled the word of God and should be prepared for the consequences. A reasonable wife who enjoys the intense love of her husband, will joyfully submit to her husband. Many marriages are suffering today because of this simple principle of submission from the wife and love from the husband. People who do not understand this principle should not marry. Marriage is avoidable, it is not compulsory.

Dear Reader, do you wish to get married? Do you understand the basic principle of love and submission?

Simply not knowing God's word, or rejecting what is said in the word, be in rebellion against it, having stubborn will, selfish desire, not willing to live the word. In the same scripture verse 26, that he may cleanse it by the washing of water by the word. To present it to himself a glorious church not having spot nor wrinkle nor any such thing that it should be holy and without blemish. Simply what God requires of his people.

It causes me to think even when a bill of divorce is rampant among Christian folks more than any other on earth. Lack of submission to God, really and truly loving God, not living a lie to say we do but yet still not keeping his word. This is so powerful that it's the true test of submission to God. Someone can easily get up and decide to break covenant with God because of self-gratification, self-will or desire, or Satan will to affect marriages of the kingdom.

Based on the levels of how people who claim to love God has taken the route to exit marriages easily without giving just cause as Jesus explained in St. Matthew 19:9. Christians really hath to go back to Calvary and check our hearts really not like Jesus; bowels of mercy and compassion; forgiving, honest, seek to esteem others above self, restoring, to die for the ones he loves. With Christ imminent return, the heart of people within the body is woefully painful.

I cried tears to see the state of many hearts and how we treat God and even our marriages. Then enemy laugh or have a field day because Christians simply fail to submit truly to God.

Let us honor God's word above all.   (1ˢᵗ Samuel 15: 22-23.)

Evangelist Patrick Smith
Banker, NCB
Kingston, (Jamaica)

OUR MARRIAGE

Our marriage was established by God on June 29, 2002. We have been married for sixteen (16) years. Like many marriages, there has been struggles; however, with Christ we were and are still able to overcome.

We believe communication is the fundamental key. Marriage issues should be openly discussed and guided through prayer.

Noel & Tasha Smith

SUCCESSFUL MARRIAGE

In order for marriage to be successful partners must accept each other for who they are, never try to change anything about your partner. If there are changes you wish to see in your partner, pray about it. When you try to play God in your wife or husband's life you are digging a pit and someone will fall in it. In other words, you are creating problems. Leave the fixing of people's life to God, he makes no mistake.

Look for the best in your partner and complement them. Let them know how wonderful they are, how gifted they are, how smart they are. Learn not to major in the minors. Tell your husband or wife that you love him/her. Never say "they know you do" remember reassuring them is very important because someone on the outside might just do it for you.

Stop taking advice from people about your marriage, remember not everyone celebrates your relationship especially when theirs are not going well. You can't ask someone who have never been married to make your marriage work, they will destroy it.

Lastly, take your partner out on date and play with each other. Change up your dress code, your hair style, have a new look and a fresh prospective of life each day. This will help you both to excel in Jesus Christ in every aspect of your life. Your marriage started with

Jesus, continue in him always being the core and the apex of your life.

Karen Gowie-Williamson (Educator)

Kingston, Jamaica

KEYS TO OUR SUCCESSFUL MARRIAGE

God, Man and Woman

Amanda and I have been married for Eleven (11) years. During these times it takes both of us to make this work.

The most important aspect of our marriage is keeping God in the middle. As long as he is in the middle then we have to go through him to get to each other. When this happens, since God is Love, when we go through him to each other, then we can only approach each other in love.

Pastor Brock & Amanda Jeffcoat

Apostle Tyrone Quick (Sr.) & Prophetess Yolanda Quick

God's Plan

I love my wife. We have been married over twenty-one (21) years.

I encourage any couple to desire to get married.

Marriage is a good thing if Christ is the center of it.

Be encouraged, marriage is God's plan.

Apostle Tyrone Quick (Sr.) & Prophetess Yolanda Quick

Communication and Fun

We have been married for eleven (11) years.

What have kept us together is communication. It wasn't easy at first but then we got the hang of it.

We also make sure we had talks on different topics, anything in particular

We have lots of fun together.

Ebonie Williams (Mrs.)
St. Catherine, Jamaica

EXPRESSION:

We have been married for three (3) years. We find the key ingredient to successful marriage is honesty. Express the importance what can do and do not do is formula for success.

Congratulations to Rev. Wisdom and his wife for thirty-six (36) years of marriage and I pray that the book – titled '**The Key to Successful Marriage**' will touch lives.

Bishop Ulysses Sullivan & Lady Carol Sullivan

Minister Alphaeus & Andrea Reid

Marriage is beautiful and honorable by God. A successful marriage as to be built on the foundation and moral that god required. Faith in God, excellent communication, support unconditional love, patience and forgiveness, respect for each other, trust honesty, attention, time saving, compatibility, understanding and intimacy are some of the attribute that makes our marriage of 18 years successful and growing strong.

Minister Alphaeus & Andrea Reid

THE STORY OF OUR MARRIAGE - David & Lynne Best Jr.

When I was younger, I once asked dad, "How will I know the right girl for me to marry? "The simple and short answer I received was, "You'll just know."

I have reflected on that answer before I was married and many times since. I'm not told it was the best advice I ever received from my dad. However, it does make sense now; Perfect sense actually. Much later in life, while on a fishing trip with my dad on the Edisto river he told me he had a lady "picked out for me ." She was a member of his church congregation and quite frankly I was intrigued. Later Lynne and I were introduced, with both of us seemingly interested in the other. The rest is as they say, "History." To indulge in a few details, I didn't believe it at first. Even more so I didn't want to trust someone else to give advice about who I might date, who my girlfriend might be, much less who I might marry. As it went down Lynne and I did date for a spell and then I broke it off. Citing concern of my working out of town, always on the road and a long-distance relationship would be tough on us. She really deserved better than I could give. I remembered her words as clearly today, as if she was speaking them now, "I'll wait on you ". Well I thought our continued relations would be unfair for both of us and that was it. Years would past from that day until the next time Lynne would be in my life and then following elderly wisdom, eventually my wife.

Our wedding day was filled with all the things of tradition; four weeks of public church service announcements of our intent be to wed, private plans of an ole timey church setting with simple, yet elegant plans and decorations were prepared. All mixed with a ton of anticipation.

The day of the ceremony was nothing less than just a hair from overwhelming. There were family and friends, support and pressure. All the goodness of our lives and past experiences we each had all packed into one little country church house- all the people who carried and shared those memories at least.

She rode in on a horse drawn carriage and her dad escorted her down the center aisle. When she entered the church that day, I remembered thinking she is the most beautiful lady I ever seen. There facing each other and then side by side we were led in our vows of matrimony. Our first act as husband and wife was holy communion taking there that day in the sight of God and of man. We wanted it to be a symbol, to all those who witnessed, of our commitment to love and serve each other, but most of all to symbolize our desire toward God of his place in our lives in our place in his.

The clergy announced us to the audience as Mr. and Mrs. David Forrest Best Jr. We locked arms and danced out of the sanctuary to the jazz tune of "In the mood." We took a celebratory carriage ride released white doves to mark the occasion and then ate cake. Since that day we have not let the excitement of our relationship dull nor the newness of it fade.

Even though life is steady and often Lynne and I have tried to live ours ~ together. We've loved together, cried together, seen loved ones pass on and new life be born, all the while – together. We don't hide our love for one another from those whom we happen to be around, especially others whom we love. We hug, we kiss, we hold hands. Our children often witness our fond affection for one another in our home and while we are out in the town. Lottie and Lee have no doubt that their daddy loves their mama and that their mama respects their daddy.

We live a real life together where we openly talk about building legacy. Conversing often of how this very moment will impact the future. All the while trying to live on purpose knowing that eternity is at stake. As our daily life is filled with work and responsibility, providing for our family and instructing our children, it has not always been easy to keep things in perspective. However, one grounding and endearing attribute of Lynne has been her quite faith and devotion toward the LORD. Many times, arriving home late from work I have entered the house to find her busy about the tasks of home-making. Cooking, cleaning and childrearing, with her bible opened on the kitchen table, flour dusting the pages, as she searches out the recipes for life, while waiting on my return.

We've stayed in church, that is to say close to where God's people gather. Learning the whole while that all walks of life are welcomed where the LORD is given reign. We haven't gotten too caught up in "religion" nor in the superstitions of man, but we have tried to allow God to guide us, many times across rough waters, to where he is. We – together – have sought to be where God would have us to be; doing what God would have us to be doing.

We've trusted each other, but trusted God more. Seeking his will for our life together. There is no competition when it comes to our individual walks with Christ. If you asked Lynne today, "Who she loves the most." She won't' say any other name but Jesus.

We have allowed Jesus to be the center of our home, not fanatically, but genuinely and for real. We've opened our home to those in need and readily confessed to each other and even to our children our failures and mishaps asking for forgiveness. Charity and forgiveness in our home has never been withheld.

We've challenged each other as we discussed, sometimes even debated, our thinking, our positions and our habits. We've often backed down, but we've never given up – that is to say never given up on each other. There has always been room in our marriage for all of us.

If you asked me today what the key to marriage is, I would have to honestly say I am really not sure I'll have to get back at you on that one as we are walking it out right now.

But I can say this, knowing who I am and far greater who's that I am has served me well. Leading my family as we serve the LORD as a family has served us well. Choosing each day to love each other while keeping in mind that love is a verb and most of all that true love is a choice. Reflecting now it is not hard to see how making ourselves right and ready with God has proved impossible without God. Because, the true expression and definition of love is displayed in and is the person of Jesus, the son of God hanging on a tree. It is by our simple faith in him, his birth, his life, his death, his resurrection and his ultimate return, that has us on the edge of our seats living life given by him – together.

With God's help this story is TO BE CONTINUED…

Pastor David & Lynne Best

**Bishop-Designate Reginald J. McLeod Sr. &
Elder Andrea R. McLeod**

My wife Elder Andrea R. McLeod and I have been married for 22 years.
My profession is that of a Senior Pastor. I have been preaching the gospel of Jesus Christ for 20 years and 18 of those years I have served as a Senior Pastor.

While there are so many things that have empowered us to have a successful marriage, I wholeheartedly believe that the primary factor that have enabled us to withstand the test of time is the fact that we quite often remind ourselves according to Ecclesiastes 4:12 that Though one may be overpowered, two can defend themselves, however a cord of three strands is not quickly broken. No matter what my wife and I have faced over the years no matter how difficult it was, we have always taken great joy and consolation in the fact that our marriage not only consists of my wife and myself but it consists of her, myself and most importantly God and therefore failure has not been and will never be an option.

**Bishop-Designate Reginald J. McLeod Sr. &
Elder Andrea R. McLeod**

CLOSING STATEMENT AND ACKNOWLEDGEMENT TO GOD

Without Him I can't do nothing, without Him my life would be in vain.
Without Him I would be drifting, like a ship without a sail.
He is my rock, my strong tower, a shelter in the time of storm.
He is the commander and chief of my life, the great captain general, my
Lord Jesus Christ.

Let me share with you my life story and testimony:
I have been saved at the age of twelve (12) years old. I was born in a large
family of twelve (12) children of two (2) godly parents, God bless their
precious souls. All children are saved and married. I am a proud Jamaican.

I am an ordained Evangelist and Minister of the Gospel and has served in various areas in
the church ministry.
- Choir member
- Sunday School Teacher/Secretary
- Executive Board Member
- Men's President
- Chairman of Prison Ministry
- Chairman of Hospitality Committee
- Organizer of Marriage Couple Seminar
- Counsellor and adviser
- Caterer and Banquet Manager
- Director of a Youth Mentoring Group

I am very excited about life and people in general. People are one of the greatest assets in
Our world.
My aim and objective of this book is that it will be a catalyst of change to its readers and the
world at large. I would like you to know that you are beautiful, you are handsome, you are
specially designed for each other. Believe in yourselves, love yourselves, give your marriage the
best treatment. Water your marriage with prayer and fasting and the Word of God. Lets
forget the ugly past and forgive each other, hold hands together look in each other eyes and
reaffirm your love and commitment. Put your hands in the hands of the Lord he is well able to
take you through the struggles, don't give up you can make it to the top.

BE BLESSED OF GOD IN ALL AREAS OF YOUR LIVE.

Rev. and Mrs. Gladstone Wisdom

Congratulations

Congratulations

Congratulations Evangelist Wisdom who have been married for Thirty- six (36) blissful years. I admired your commitment and dedication to your family and church. You displayed patience, boldness, strictness, humbleness and honesty in your leadership.

For your successful marriage, both partners have shown unending patience and forgiveness to each other, especially in times of trials.

You communicated as much as possible and trust each other. Most importunately, as you spend quality time together in your relationship also as you followed the principles of the Bible especially Genesis 2:24. This has cemented your relationship to be a successful one.

Sonia Wilks

Congratulations

I am honored to be allowed this space to be able to send words of congratulations to one of the world's best couple. I've been blessed with the opportunity of getting to know you both for over six (6) years and the love, affection, strength, courage, trust and respect that you both have displayed to this union. It leads a lasting impact to my life; the encouragement that marriages still last, that person of different character can come together and through love put aside selfishness and still be subjected to one partner. Your union has still offer hope to many other unions, the hope that this thing can work.

Today so many marriages have died, and this dead rate continues to rise, but like a light on dark night so is the life of your union. It continues to shine it light of hope.

Congratulations to you both on your 36 years of togetherness. The blessings of the lord continue with you to the end of your life journey.

Raphel & Shellyann Wisdom

Congratulations

Congratulations, Evangelist and mother Wisdom, on your wedding anniversary. Together you are an inspiration to a life lived energetically and passionately, and pursuit of the LORD. May your life together not be a blessing today, but a continued blessing on generations to come, for the glory of God and the expanding of his Kingdom.

With heartfelt sincerity

David Best & Family

Congratulations

I do take this opportunity to congratulate Rev. Gladstone Wisdom and his beautiful wife of 36 years on this a landmark achievement of togetherness and many years to come

Minister Alphaeus & Andrea Reid

Congratulations

Rev. Gladstone Wisdom has been a tower of strength and an inspiration for as long as I known him. His wealth of knowledge and successful marriage is evident in his life and this he shares with everyone who cross his path.

I am truly a recipient of his ministry as I always remembered the many encouragement, I received on allowing God to have first place in my life and to depend totally on the Lord when seeking a Godly husband.

Rev. Wisdom desire to give back can help you achieve a successful marriage through the lessons he shares in this book.

Claudia Mitchell

Congratulations

This is a true statement about Rev. Gladstone Wisdom. I have known him for twenty-seven (27) years. He is a true believer of good. He always greets you with the word of God. "God bless you Sis. Reynolds, God love you." "No man doesn't give up, just hold on to your God." "God is faithful, stay right in there."

He always wears a smile on his face. He maintains a Godly lifestyle. He has one wife, he loves to preach the word of God and he serves the church well.

He is a good person, well appreciative and stands for good principles. He is trustworthy.

Rev. Wisdom is a true man of God.

Audrey Reynolds

Congratulations

Rev. Wisdom is a great contributor to the works of the Lord and ambassador to the kingdom of God. He is a truly and inspiration to me for some years. A dedicated man of God, A father and a husband. I'll like to congratulate you and your wife for keeping it (your marriage together all these years). You are truly an example to all the persons you have come in contact with. You have influenced my life immensely. Every time I feel like compromising in areas where I shouldn't, I remember Kind words telling me, I am precious, I am Gods temple and not to settle for less than deserve.

You are a true oracle of the Most High God and I love.

Nicole Innis

Congratulations

I have known Pastor Gladstone Wisdom for over 7 years and over these years my respect for him has grown. He is genuine, committed and honest. He found me in my lowest state and encouraged me back to life. He adopted, protected and fathered me faithfully over these years.

His value for relations and his pursuit to see people restored is truly evident in his character. He carries the aroma of one who is redeemed and set apart and have imparted these traits in my life.

Shashawna Williams

Congratulations

I have known Rev. Wisdom for over five (5) years. Within these years that I have known him he always has some encouraging words to offer.

Rev. Wisdom will be like "Pauline did you go to church on Sunday"? He would ask about your relationship and encourages by saying to you that marriage is sacred and ordained by God.

It is a joy to congratulate you and your soulmate, your best friend, your God – given gift for achieving thirty – six (36) years of marriage.

May Gods blessings continue to be upon your lives. You have been a good example.

Pauline Barrett

Congratulations

To a true servant of the Lord Jesus Christ. Congratulations to you my dear friend, you have always been a tower of strength in the lives of people especially the ones that are hurting more. Somehow you have a way of captivating the ones who some would pass by. Your undying love for the work of God have created an avenue for reaching the Lost at any cost. Your spread the word of God through your work on T- shirts, through book markers, through brochures using bible scriptures and know you are doing a book! To God be the glory.

This a milestone only God could have created this avenue for you. You have toiled long and hard; your kind words, your smile, your never-ending pushes have only strengthened you more to do the work of God just to reach a soul, that need to hear someone say, "I love you", a soul that sometimes thinks no one cares. You specialize also in reaching married couples, the single who are in touch relationships; you always have an encouraging word for us.

Thank you for your perseverance, you believe that you can make a difference in people's lives and I believe you have done well. To God be the glory! Go forth with power and strength. Congratulations also to you and Lady Wisdom on celebrating 36 years of marriage. I know it wasn't easy but through it all you have learned to trust the lord. God bless you as you continue on this new walk.

Blessing and love.

Minister Dahalia Chevannes- Henry

Congratulations

To his hand-picked couple celebrating Thirty-six (36) glorious years of marriage. I know it wasn't easy but because you both trust in confident God; he has kept you going. You are an exemplary couple with a reputation second to none. I am proud of you both and I know the same God will continue to see you through to the end of life. Thirty- six (36) years is not chicken, it is mother hen, we know what mother hen does, she nurtures, protect and provide. As you continue on this journey with the passion that you have for successful marriage, I want to join in and say, one can give and don't love, but you cannot love and don't give. It is same way a marriage cannot survive without forgiveness.

For you to have reached Thirty -six (36) years I don't have to ask what the ingredients is. It must be love and of course when teeth and tongue meet it is Solve with forgiveness. God bless you both and hope that you will live and enjoy Thirty – six (36) more glorious years of togetherness.
Rev. Portia Blair

Congratulations

Congratulations to a wonderful couple, Mr. & Mrs. Wisdom who have celebrated thirty-six (36) years of marriage within the Kingdom of God. They have been a great blessing to the body of Christ. Not only are they married for 36 years, but they are also a born again believers and have been proclaiming the Gospel of Christ over these years.

Having met this wonderful couple almost ten (10) years ago through an annual Marriage Conference hosted by my wife and I. They quickly became a part of the conference and gave their support to enhance the Kingdom of God. This too, has been an important area for them, as they have also hosted similar Marriage Banquet.

Rev. Wisdom and I shared great moments and conversations, especially along the line of marriage, as this area means much to us and God. I have shared prophetic words over his life and the Lord has blessed him tremendously. **To God be the glory.**

It is an honor to be a part of something great and mean much to my friend and brother. May God bless this book and all the **readers.**

Patrick Smith (Evangelist)
Kingston, Jamaica.

Congratulations

I am a High School Spanish Teacher who loves the Lord. I have known Rev. Wisdom for over two (2) years. He is very jovial, kind, caring forgiving and gives great advice. I congratulate him and his wife for achieving, only with God's help, thirty-six (36) years of marriage and I pray God's continued assistance to achieve many more loving years.

I thank God for giving Rev. Wisdom the initiative and mandate to write this book for the purpose of inspiring married couples to stand strong through challenges, enjoy the joys of marriage and glorify God through the ministry of Marriage. Knowing well, that this institution is designed by God and must be kept out of the hands of the enemy, who seeks to destroy anything created by God the Father.

Toni Ann Duffus
St. Catherine, Jamaica

Congratulations

Evangelist Wisdom is a man who is exemplifies the scripture, "redeeming the time for the days are evil." He expresses his heart to the listener within the limitations of time and space. He loves God and God's people. He seeks to edify God's people daily. I believe this book will loose chains that the enemy has placed on some Christian marriages.

Wanda Woods
Bennettsville, South Carolina.

Congratulations

What an amazing accomplishment to be married for thirty-six (36) years. I can't imagine the things the two of you went through and the strength of your bond. This is truly wonderful and I hope one day to be able to say the same.

Congratulations and best wishes with your new book.

Klay Kennedy
Bennettsville, South Carolina.

Congratulations

Husbands, love your wives, just as Christ loved the church and gave himself up for her to make her holy, cleansing her by the washing with water through the word, and to present her to himself as a radiant church, without stain or wrinkle or any other blemish, but holy and blameless.

In the same way, husbands ought to love their wives as their own bodies. He who loves his wife loves himself. After all, no one ever hated their own body, but they feed and care for their body, just as Christ does the church – for we are members of his body. For this reason, a man will leave his father and mother and be united to his wife, and the two will become one flesh.   **Ephesians 5:25-31.**

Harry Easterling Jr,
South Carolina

Congratulations

Congratulations to Rev. Gladstone Wisdom on responding to the call and assuming the task of writing this timely book, "**The Key to a Successful Marriage.**"

Recognizing the challenges placed on the sanctity of marriage, it is my hope that this book will greatly impact and radically transform marriages to reflect God's plan. It is also my prayer that it will provide a guide to anyone embarking on the worthy estate of matrimony.

Beverly Barrett
Philadelphia, Pennsylvania.

Congratulations

We have been happily married for thirty-eight (38) years. God is the head of my life and also the family. There are two (2) keys that kept us over the years which is Prayer and Faith.

I extend heartiest congratulations to Rev. & Mrs. Wisdom for celebrating thirty-six (36) years of Marriage and also the writing of the book 'The Key to Successful Marriage'.

Pastor James & Tawanka Smith
Bennettsville, South Carolina.

Congratulations

Heartiest congratulations Rev. Wisdom on the completion of your book 'The Key to a Successful Marriage'. Your experience for thirty-six (36) years of marriage is a dream, passion and vision come through. God bless you both.
Rev. Veronica Ewan.
Kingston, Jamaica

Congratulations

Reverend Wisdom congratulations... your dream is now a reality! Hard work, dedication, determination, enthusiasm, family, friends and your faith in God have been the 'key elements' for the success of your book, "The Key to a Successful Marriage."..I can remember the first time (about four years ago you shared your dream of writing this book and even showed me your first rough draft, and now it's a complete book!... already I'm looking forward to its sequel...
God has blessed you and your wife with 37 grand years of marriage...I'm sure this book will be of great value to singles, those planning to get married and those who are already married...May the good LORD continue to bless and keep
you and your family...

Your friend and sister in Christ Jesus
Alicia Archibald
Kingston, Jamaica

Congratulations

I take this privilege to say congratulations to the Wisdoms on their thirty-six (36) years of marriage and togetherness. Many declare that they are married but they are not together. They sleep in separate rooms and have separate aspirations or competing with each other. I know the Wisdoms for over twenty (20) years and I can say they are a living example of what marriage should be.

Congratulations on this drive to educate others on how they can let their marriage please God and others.

Karen Gowie-Williamson
Kingston, Jamaica.

Congratulations

Marriage is a blessing when God is in the center. The more we love God is the better husbands & wives we become. Understanding the 5 Love Languages plays a very important role identifying your partner's love language which will lead to a successful marriage. Always remember that a marriage is never a one-way street, it works both ways, compromising in love.

Congratulations to my Dad & Mom on achieving such a great milestone of 36 years in marriage. I believe this book with so many experiences of marriages with help many tomorrows understand the key to a successful marriage.

Gailon & Roxanne Wisdom

Congratulations

Congratulations to Rev. Gladstone Wisdom on responding to the call and assuming the task of writing this timely book, "The Key To A Successful marriage".
Recognizing the challenges placed on the sanctity of marriage, it is my hope that this book will greatly impact and radically transform marriages to reflect God's plan. It is also my prayer that it will provide a guide to anyone embarking on the worthy estate of matrimony.

B. Barrett
Philadelphia, Pennsylvania

Congratulations

I just want to congratulate my dear Cousin Gladstone, on writing a book on marriage.

What is wonderful Gladstone has a successful marriage of over 30+ years!
He is also a devoted Christian who uses the bible as his compass....

From the bible's perspective...Marriage is the union of a man and women as husband and wife according to the standard set out by God.
Marriage is a divine institution, authorized and established by God In Eden.
Marriage brings into being the family unite the family circle.

Marriage was designed to form a permanent bond of union between man and women that they might be mutually helpful to each other.
Living together in love and confidence, they could enjoy great happiness.

Once again congratulations for having the 3-way cord...God. Yourself and your wife.
A twist is easily unraveled compared to a braid or plait.

Agape love...
Janice Dunkley
London UK.

Congratulations

I got married in 1984 fairly young. I renewed my vow to serve the Lord shortly after.
As a teacher our living standards were exemplary in and out of the classroom so being a Christian helped me to display these qualities.
I was the primary breadwinner since my spouse was a small farmer. I tried to make ends meet leaning on the Lord to supply our needs rearing two boys.
The Lord blessed us early in the marriage with a home and other things needed. My Husband wasn't a believer but he didn't hinder me from going to church and perform duties I had to do even those which took me away from home quite often. He was a disciplinarian so the boys had to be in order which made it easier for us.
God was the forefront in my marriage because on many occasions problems occurred which could cause even divorce. My faith and trust in God

anchored me so we could overcome the problems. It took hard work and dedication and love to have come this far. To God be the glory for these 36 years of marriage.

Mrs. Clara Wisdom McIntosh
Jamaica

Congratulations

Congratulations Mom & Dad on 36 years of marriage. Thank you for being a great example to your son and I. It's an honor to have you two as our parents. We admired the people you are, kind, loving, and God fearing. Thank you for being opened and honest about what marriage entails the good, bad, and sometimes ugly. We appreciate all the great advice you give us as a newlywed. We love you both, and pray for God's riches blessing on your lives.

Gavin & Sherika Wisdom

Congratulations

It is with profound joy that I congratulate you Rev Gladstone Wisdom on the authorship of your book - The Key to a successful marriage. I am proud to have been a recipient of your love, and ministry to the Church for over twenty years. Your marriage and relationship with Jesus Christ have truly been an example of good works and a light and beacon that have guided many to same successful path to marriage and holistic living. You and your lovely wife Mrs. Valerie Wisdom are truly amazing gifts to the body of Christ. May your book touch the lives of many and to every heart that receives its message may it bring exponential blessings that will flow into the lives of others.

Much love and blessings to you.

Jeneva Allen
Tax Education Officer
Tax Administration Jamaica
West Indies

Congratulations

I have known Reverend Wisdom for over twenty years now and one thing I can say about his personality trait is that it has been very consistent throughout the years and as his name suggest he is a Wise man. His wisdom surpasses that of his peers and colleagues, which I consider to be one that is divinely inspired by God. He boasts thirty-six years of marriage and is now a grandfather.

He is a great man of God who is very passionate about evangelism and ministry as a whole. He inspires one to worship our God and does the same with enthusiasm. He epitomizes the spirit of servanthood while he leads with humility. Rev Wisdom has great social skills and is a people person. He seeks after all he knows; he does not follow the masses but formulates his own opinion of an individual even if it goes against that of those around him. He is never afraid to stand alone and maintain his stance on any issue or topic of discussion.

He is a great family man who provides the best care and support to his children and wife. This affection does not stop with his family but goes beyond to all the families he comes in contact with. He checks in to ensure relationships are what they should be and in the event they are not, he offers family counselling to remedy the situation.

He displays high morals which command the respect of all who comes in contact with him. His business ethics and administrative skills are impeccable and he is highly influential. He is a motivator who constantly reminds you of your potential and the goals you set and ensure you take the necessary steps to achieve and realize these goals.

With these admirable qualities and the experiences Reverend Wisdom has garnered over the years, he indeed has the authority to speak through writing on the topic of "A Successful Marriage." Considering the times, we are in where marriages are constantly going under, I endorse his right to speak on this matter. I pray that through his inspiration this book will touch all God intended it to touch and family lives over the world will be transformed as a result.

Every Blessing Reverend Wisdom!!!!!
Suzette Douglas
Your sister in the Ministry of Christ.

Congratulations

"They key to successful marriage" is a great topic. I know it will have a great impact on young couples. Blessings coming from JM Portmore, St. Catherine.

Rev. Wisdom very kind hearted, up beat in is Christian walk with God, always giving encouragement. One who love God very deeply, always boasting about the Lord God Almighty.

Never a dull moment in his presence. Very straight forward individual, always giving a listening ear and out stretched arms. A shoulder to cry on, when face with overwhelmed situations.

A counselor you can relate to and share, your personal challenges. Rev. Wisdom gives you biblical counseling session to your situation.

Rev. Wisdom is very respectful, family oriented God fearing, man of purpose.

I am very, very blessed to have Rev. Wisdom in my life as a very good and dear friend.

Congratulations to Rev. & Sister Wisdom. Wow for those long, long, long years.

Mighty God of Daniel 36yrs of Marriage. Indeed, what God joins together is rock solid, no devil in hell cannot interfere.

Continue to place God at the fore front of your marriage. As you both journey along to the next level, the next chapter. God blessings and favors be granted throughout your life time together.

May the Lord bless you, and keep you, cause His face to shine upon you, and be gracious onto you. May He lift His countenance upon you. And give you peace both now and forever
Love Careen

Congratulations for the lounging of this Beautiful Book:

The Key to Successful Marriage. May the Lord God Almighty continue to download and deposit in his Spirit the wisdom as his name suggest, knowledge and understand to accomplish many more inspirational Books on marriage.
Congratulations once again blessings.

For the wonderful work you have done, by making yourself available to be used as a vessel. And to be plyer able in God hand. Indeed, God is the Potter and you are the clay, as He mold and shape you for greatness.

Bless up love you

Congratulations

I want to send special greetings to the wisdom family and more life on their anniversary.
Rev Wisdom is like a father to me he always looks out for me, guide me and send his love and prayers for myself and my family. I have known him for more than 5 years he never stops encouraging young, older and the indifference. I'm grateful to have him has a father figure and friend. Bless you.

Chevane Trowers

Congratulations

We wish to use this medium to congratulate the Wisdoms – Gladstone & Valerie on thirty-six (36) years of Marriage **"to have and to hold."** This is indeed a milestone. Also, we wish to congratulate them both on this distinguished achievement of writing their first book. The Benderson' salute you both for the wonderful example set for those coming after you.

Marlon & Carmelita Benderson
St. Catherine, Jamaica.

Congratulations

We would like to congratulate Gladstone & Valerie Wisdom on the milestone that you have accomplished thirty-six (36) years of togetherness. We wish for you another 36 years and more, you have set an example for us. Gods richest blessings to you both.

Granville and Desserene Benjamin
(Educator)

Congratulations

Congratulations Rev. & Mrs. Wisdom on thirty-six (36) years and also on this wonderful book of marriage.

Pastor Larry & Libbie Baldwin

Congratulations

Congratulations to Reverend Gladstone and Valerie Wisdom on thirty-six (36) years of marriage. In the years of rising divorces and separations, this in itself is quite a testimony.

Pastor Joseph & Rosella James

Congratulations

I wish to extend my profound Congratulation to Rev. Wisdom on your new book, titled '**The Key to Successful Marriage.**' The book is long overdue and I also want to thank you for the privilege granted to me in making my contribution as it relates to the title of your book.

Paula McCreath- Wright

Congratulations Reverend Wisdom
on your new book

My name is **Monique Clarke** and I am from Jamaica, and I think Reverend Wisdom is a very hardworking, inspirational and passionate individual, and I admire his passion to win souls for God, and I think that is a very outstanding and lovely man of God. I love his ability to motivate individuals with his special words of wisdom and motivation. I think he is very intelligent and powerful when he ministers to persons and I think he is very successful in all his endeavours. Congratulations on your thirty six years of marriage and congratulations on your amazing book which has the name the key to a successful marriage and I know that it is a book that everyone will really enjoy because your ministry is so precious. Thank you for writing this book and may God continue to bless your soul richly.

SPECIAL THANKS

A special thanks to all the sponsors and friends who have helped me in one way or another. May your life, business and families be blessed beyond measures.

It is my prayer and hope that your life will be challenged and blessed and that you will move to a higher dimension in your marriage. I trust that you will be a tremendous blessing to others and to the kingdom of God.

Rev. Gladstone Wisdom

Made in the USA
Columbia, SC
10 September 2020